The Poetry Of Dante's Inferno

A. Gaspary

Kessinger Publishing's Rare Reprints

Thousands of Scarce and Hard-to-Find Books
on These and other Subjects!

- Americana
- Ancient Mysteries
- Animals
- Anthropology
- Architecture
- Arts
- Astrology
- Bibliographies
- Biographies & Memoirs
- Body, Mind & Spirit
- Business & Investing
- Children & Young Adult
- Collectibles
- Comparative Religions
- Crafts & Hobbies
- Earth Sciences
- Education
- Ephemera
- Fiction
- Folklore
- Geography
- Health & Diet
- History
- Hobbies & Leisure
- Humor
- Illustrated Books
- Language & Culture
- Law
- Life Sciences

- Literature
- Medicine & Pharmacy
- Metaphysical
- Music
- Mystery & Crime
- Mythology
- Natural History
- Outdoor & Nature
- Philosophy
- Poetry
- Political Science
- Science
- Psychiatry & Psychology
- Reference
- Religion & Spiritualism
- Rhetoric
- Sacred Books
- Science Fiction
- Science & Technology
- Self-Help
- Social Sciences
- Symbolism
- Theatre & Drama
- Theology
- Travel & Explorations
- War & Military
- Women
- Yoga
- *Plus Much More!*

We kindly invite you to view our catalog list at:
www.kessinger.net

II

THE POETRY OF THE INFERNO

BY ADOLF GASPARY.[1]

DANTE'S poem describes to us a spiritual journey. It passes from place to place, continually changing the scenery and the characters of the drama; one single person always remains, Dante, the traveler himself. In the Commedia the greatest subjectivity rules supreme: the poet himself never leaves the scene of action, he is the hero of the action, the most interesting figure in it, and all that he sees and learns awakens a living echo in his emotional soul. He speaks with the sinners, the penitents, and saints, and in these conversations he paints himself. But for a journey on so grand a scale every conceivable space must needs be limited, even that of the longest poem. An enormous number of persons appears and disappears in this poem. The reader is continually hurried onwards from one to the other: there is little time for each, and a few traits must suffice to sketch his portrait. The great scenes are developed almost casually, or, rather, there is no space for their development, so rapidly does the narrative progress. In this way Dante's Inferno,

---

[1] *The History of Early Italian Literature to the Death of Dante,* Adolf Gaspary, trans. by Herman Oelsner, M. A., Ph. D. George Bell & Sons, London. The extracts from this valuable book are made through the courteous permission of the translator, Dr. Oelsner.

especially, is a very whirlwind of emotions, passions, and events. If it had not been a Dante that was creating them, the poetical situation would have been destroyed and the figures stifled, the work becoming dry and empty owing to the superabundance of the subject-matter. But Dante possesses the art of drawing his figures even in a limited space. At times they remain sketches, though sketches by a master hand; but frequently the few traits suffice to bring before our mind the entire and complete picture, with all its details. Dante is the great master of poetic expression: with his energetic style, he is able to condense a world of ideas and feelings in a single word, in an image that carries us away and places us in the midst of the situation.

At the very beginning of the Commedia, in the midst of the thorny allegories, the reader is fascinated by the sympathetic figure of Virgil, and by the gentle opening conversation between him and his charge. The fourth canto describes the privileged sojourn of the great heathens in Limbo, and expresses in a most fascinating manner Dante's deep reverence for antiquity, and, at the same time, the consciousness he has of his own merit, when he tells how he was himself introduced by Virgil into the circle of the five great poets as a sixth. He felt that he was destined to revive an art that had been so long lost, and just pride such as this pleases us in the case of a man of genius. The general impression of this situation is vivid, — the noble gathering, all the heroes and sages, and, in their midst, their great admirer and disciple. But the individual figures are not yet clearly distinguished; the poet gives little more than a number of names, rarely adding an epithet or a circumstance that might characterize the man. It is a kind of catalogue, and not even the usual *et cetera* of such enumerations is missing (iv. 145) : —

Io non posso ritrar di tutti appieno.

This same method, which is, as it were, an abbreviated form of true poetic exposition, is continued in the following canto. Here the poet has reached the second circle, that of the carnal sinners, who are driven to and fro by a raging tempest. Among them he sees Semiramis, Dido, Cleopatra, Helen, Achilles, Paris, Tristan, *e più di mille*. But these enumerations of Dante's are merely introductory : from the bands of spirits, forming the general background, single ones detach themselves. Among these souls, two that are borne along together by the wind specially attract his attention. They are Francesca of Rimini and her Paolo, who, burning for each other with sinful love, were slain by Gianciotto Malatesta, Lord of Rimini, Francesca's husband, and the brother of Paolo. Dante does not know them, but the pair, united even in the torments of Hell, arouse his sympathy; he would fain speak with them, and obtains his guide's permission. This is one of the passages in which the special character of Dante's poetry is best revealed. Many persons, nowadays, who have heard the famous Francesca da Rimini so much discussed, may perhaps feel somewhat disappointed when they open the book. There are scarcely seventy verses, which are quickly read, and which leave but little impression on the ordinary and superficial reader. A sensitive mind is needed for the appreciation of Dante's condensed poetry. It is to be found in each small detail, in every syllable, — nothing is empty and devoid of meaning, but much remains dumb to him who hurries over the verses.

Acting on Virgil's advice, Dante entreats the two souls by the love that binds them together, and they follow the sympathetic call —

> As turtle doves, called onward by desire,
> With open and steady wings to the sweet nest
> Fly through the air by their volition borne.

This gentle image, taken from the Æneid, but imbued by Dante with a more intimate spirit, serves as a preparation for the moving scene. This very trait of their immediately following the call that is directed to their love, and even more so the first words of the reply, characterize the two figures. Francesca's is a noble and tender soul, and the sympathy shown her by a stranger moves her deeply in her pain. In her gratitude, she would fain pray for him to the King of the Universe; but she is in Hell, and her entreaties are not heard in Heaven. She will at least fulfill his wish by answering him. She tells him who they are, by indicating their native place, and above all by speaking of that which has brought them down there, their unexampled and boundless love. In seven lines is contained the whole history of their feelings. Each *terzina* begins with the word "love;" each one describes to us the growth of its power, and shows us how it arises in the man's heart on beholding the beautiful woman, how it is kindled in the heart of the woman when she sees herself loved, how it becomes their common fate and hurries them to one common doom. When Dante has heard this, he can no longer doubt who the two are, whose destiny has been so powerfully affected by love, and his second question begins with the name Francesca, although she has not told it him.   But first he relapses into a deep silence, and bows his head, so that his guide asks him of what he is thinking.   The few words he has heard enable him to imagine all the feelings, joys, and sorrows they conceal, and he turns to her again with a deeper interest : —

> Thine agonies, Francesca,
> Sad and compassionate to weeping make me.
> But tell me, at the time of those sweet sighs,
> By what and in what manner Love conceded,
> That you should know your dubious desires ?

Dante puts this question of his in the tenderest manner, for it would be intrusive if prompted by curiosity and not by sympathy.   But Francesca at once detects the latter quality, and therefore she will answer, although the recollection gives her pain : —

> Farò come colui che piange e dice.[1]

This passage has often been compared with that other one, apparently so similar, at the beginning of Ugolino's narrative (Inf. xxxiii. 4), in order to show the consummate mastery with which Dante was able to depict his various characters, even outwardly, by the sound of the verses.   Here in Francesca's speech all is soft and harmonious, in Ugolino's all is rough and hard ; in the one all is love, in the other rage and fury.   It gives Ugolino pain, as it did Francesca, to speak of the past ; but Francesca speaks because she notes Dante's sympathy, Ugolino because he desires to revenge himself on his enemy.   Francesca

---

[1] I will do even as he who weeps and speaks.

scarcely speaks of her enemy, only distantly, and in
the most moving manner she alludes to her violent
death: Caina awaits him, who killed her and Paolo
— that is all. She does not even name him, she does
not think of him: she does not hate, but loves. She
tells of her love, of her joys, and of the happy time
that was happy though sinful. One day they read
of Lancelot's love ; they were alone and without
suspicion. Their eyes met several times, and their
cheeks colored, —

> But one point only was it that o'ercame us.

The passion is there ; but it is still slumbering, con-
cealed in the heart, and on beholding itself, as it were,
in a mirror, it recognizes and becomes conscious of
itself, and bursts forth suddenly in a mighty flame.
When they read how the queen was kissed by Lance-
lot, Paolo kissed her mouth, all trembling —

> That day no farther did we read therein.

While she is speaking these words, the other soul,
Paolo, silently accompanies her words with tears.
The poet lets her alone speak: for the lament of un-
happy love is more touching from the lips of a woman.
The short narrative ends with the catastrophe of the
passion. Free play is left to the excited imagination,
and Dante, a passionate nature, who has experienced
the tempests of the heart, is so full of sympathy for
them, that he sinks to the ground, " as a dead body
falls."

And this scene must be imagined in the surround-
ings of Hell, in the midst of the darkness and of
the raging and howling tempest — a contrast that in-
creases its power. It is the romance of **love** in its

greatest simplicity, but combined with all the emo-
tional elements that make a deep impression on the
mind.   The dominant feeling, that of boundless love,
is expressed in traits that are rapid, but full of sig-
nificance.   By their love are the two spirits conjured,
and they come.   Their love continues undiminished
even in the midst of such agony — "it does not yet
desert me," says Francesca — and together they are
carried along by the wind, united in punishment, as
they were in happiness.   Their love was their sin.
For him who is condemned, the sin lasts to all eter-
nity, and so their love is eternal.   It is their guilt,
but there is consolation in it, too —

Questi, che mai da me non fia diviso.[1]

In the sixth canto of the Inferno, among the glut-
tons who are tortured in the third circle of Hell, Dante
meets the Florentine Ciacco, who prophesies to him
the sad destiny of his native town.   In the seventh
canto, the two wanderers are with the avaricious and
prodigal in the fourth circle, and here Virgil addresses
to Dante the famous lines describing Fortune, an an-
gelic creature like the others, and set by God among
men, in order to preserve equality among them, and to
let worldly passions pass from one hand to another, as
justice demands.   In the fifth circle, as they are cross-
ing the Stygian marsh containing the wrathful, in
Phlegyas' boat, the meeting with Filippo Argenti takes
place.   This is narrated with bitter hatred and thirst
for vengeance, pointing not merely to moral indigna-
tion on the part of the poet, but to personal enmity.
In order to enable Dante and Virgil to enter the city

---

[1] This one, who ne'er from me shall be divided.

of Dis, which occupies the lower portion of Hell from the sixth circle, the "messenger of Heaven" (*del ciel messo*) appears in the ninth canto; this is a poetical creation of great distinction, a figure biblical in its grandeur, introduced from the outset with the sublimest images. The angel is girt with mystery, which is expressed by Virgil's hints at the end of the eighth canto and by the interrupted words at the beginning of the ninth. Virgil does not say who is coming, nor how he is coming, nor who has sent him. All these are circumstances which we do not learn; he who is coming is such a one as will open the gate of the city, it is some one that will bring aid. This mystery excites the imagination, and we remain in suspense; we expect something extraordinary and are not disappointed. Now he comes. His steps are accompanied by a boisterous sound, terrible as the roar of a tempest. The banks of the marsh tremble; before the angel's heavenly purity, before his awe-inspiring majesty, everything flees that is not pure. The damned souls hide themselves like frogs before a snake; the sinner cannot endure the sight of what is heavenly. And he goes onward; the misery and hideousness of the abyss do not affect him, he remains pure and radiant in that darkness, he does not defile himself in that filth. Dante, on seeing him, is seized with an unwonted feeling. He turns to Virgil and would fain speak and question him, but is made by him to keep silence and bow down. This is the time, not for curiosity, but for reverence; one must be silent and devout, humbly receiving the benefit of Divine grace. When the devils behold the messenger of Heaven, they resist no longer; his staff suffices to open the gates. He reproves the stubborn ones, and turns back without speaking to the poets. This sudden turning back is a movement of incomparable impressiveness. His office is at an end, the gate stands open and he tarries no longer; the things that surround him do not attract his attention, and he turns his back without casting a look, not because he despises those whom he has protected, but because his mind is wholly taken up with other matters. As mysteriously as he came, the messenger of Heaven disappears; but the effect of his presence remains. Before there was excitement, fighting, and threats. He comes, and immediately all opposition is at an end; he goes, and peace reigns supreme, and calmly the two poets enter the flaming city. Each action shows us the greatness of this figure; but the chief effect is produced by the contrast between the purity and majesty on the one hand, and on the other the lowliness and vileness of the place, when he comes, inspiring terror over the turbid waters, traversing the hideous marsh dry-shod, with the movement of his hand keeping the thick air from his countenance, accustomed as it is to the light of the spheres, and then returning full of majesty along the "dirty road." Here we have the appearance of Heaven in the midst of Hell — a situation unparalleled in its sublimity, such as, since the Bible, only Dante's powerful imagination has been able to conceive.

In the tenth canto two powerful scenes are intertwined. Here Dante finds, among the heretics who lie in fiery graves, Farinata degli Uberti, the head of the Ghibellines and a political opponent of his ancestors, who were driven from Florence by him. While they speak together their anger is kindled, and in their rapid dialogue is aroused all the old hatred of the parties that rent asunder the cities of Italy. But while Farinata, after a cutting assertion of the other speaker, is filled with sorrow at the triumph of his enemies and relapses into silence for a time, though his subsequent reply is no less bitter, the shadow of Guido Cavalcanti's father, Cavalcante, rises up. He recognizes Dante, and is surprised not to see his own son with him. Then, as an ambiguous word in the poet's speech has made him believe that his son is dead, he sinks back, overcome by grief: —

> Supin ricadde e più non parve fuora,[1]

a verse that depicts in a wonderful manner the emotion of the father, as also the proud and passionate spirit of the great Ghibelline, and his long and silent reflections, during which he has heeded nothing that is going on around him, so that he begins again as though there had been no lapse of time. This period of silence another would have left unoccupied or filled with indifferent matter. Not so Dante: between his own concluding word and the word of Farinata that takes up the dialogue again, he intercalates the whole deep story of fatherly grief. This shows us again the condensed power of Dante's poetry: in this passage of a hundred verses such a variety of emotions assail our mind in turn, that time and calm reflection are essential if we would receive a clear and complete impression of the whole. And yet, if we try to imagine something of less weight, between the two portions of the conversation with Farinata, than the episode of

---

[1] Supine
He fell again, and forth appeared no more.

Cavalcanti, we shall find that the passage would have
lost considerably in effect.   The more significant and
touching the traits that precede, the more expressive
is the impassibility of that magnanimous man, who
was occupied only with his own grief, and —

did not his aspect change,
Neither his neck did move, nor bent his side.

The meetings with Pier della Vigna and with Bru-
netto Latini in the seventh circle, that of the violent,
I shall mention only in passing; on the other hand, I
shall examine more closely Dante's originality from
another point of view.   The eighth circle of Hell,
that of the deceivers, which consists of ten concentric
valleys, spanned by rocky arches in the manner of
bridges, was named by the poet *Malebolge* ("Evil
Pouches") — a sarcastic expression instead of "sor-
rowful pits."   And these pits are indeed very sorrow-
ful; they are the place for the most odious crimes,
the place for mockery and invective.   Higher up
Dante had, it is true, also been bitter and sarcastic,
when he was standing by Farinata, and his political
passions and wounded family pride were aroused.   In
spite of this, however, he remained full of reverence
and admiration for that high-souled man, before whom
Hell itself appears to sink down when he raises him-
self from his tomb.   But now he no longer feels any
reverence: his satire becomes terrible and relentless,
being directed against things which he detests most.

The other world, set against this world of ours,
generally ends by criticising and satirizing it, as was
usual even in the earlier legends; but the true place
for the satirical element is the lower regions of Hell.
The sins that are punished in the upper circles may be

combined with magnanimity and with tenderness of
soul. Dante is compelled, by moral conviction, to
place in Hell Francesca, Farinata, Cavalcante, Pier
della Vigna, and even his fatherly friend Brunetto
Latini. But he does not reprove and mock them; on
the contrary, he feels deeply for them in their tor-
ments, loves and admires them, and immortalizes their
sympathetic figures in the episodes depicted. He does
not conceal or excuse their sin; but this sin is of such
a kind that it does not touch their character. Other
vices, on the other hand, according to Dante, affect
the entire personality of the man, destroy human na-
ture itself, and but rarely leave room for nobler quali-
ties. These sinners are, therefore, detestable beings;
their case must be met not by compassion, but by re-
lentless justice: here mockery and contempt are called
for. With these the last two circles are almost en-
tirely filled. We say " almost " advisedly: for even
here there is not an utter lack of greatness in all the
figures, and we cannot but admire the bold Ulysses,
and sympathize with Ugolino, while he fills us with ter-
ror. Poetry revolts against the systematic strictness
of logic. It is not a religious and philosophical trea-
tise with which we are dealing, and the vivid imagi-
nation of the poet, in these portions of the poem as
always, traverses the entire gamut of human feelings.

Dante's satirical power is at its height when he
encounters Pope Nicholas III. among the simonists
(Inf. xix.). The Pope is in a pit in the third
bolgia, his head stuck in foremost, and his burning
soles jutting out. Whilst he painfully moves his
legs to and fro in the air, he has to listen to Dante's
words of reproof and mockery : ——

> Whoe'er thou art, that standest upside down,
> O doleful soul, implanted like a stake . . .

With these expressions of contempt the poet begins his discourse. He then compares him with a murderer, who is buried alive, and who, in order to put off his death for a short while, calls again for the confessor; the murderer is the Pope, and the confessor, Dante. But the bitterest mockery the poet placed in the sinner's own mouth, when he confesses in such a way that his words become a satire against himself:—

> Know that I vested was with the great mantle,

he begins; but scarcely is there time for reverence for the highest dignity on earth to be awakened, when he adds how he defiled it, thus changing the nascent feeling to one of loathing:—

> And truly was I son of the She-bear,
> So eager to advance the cubs, that wealth
> Above, and here myself, I pocketed.

This ironical allusion to the Pope's family name (Orsini), and the play on the word *borsa*, which, in its rapidity, has a sharp point, become all the more effective from the fact that he has to utter the words himself. Nicholas III. was dead in the year of the vision; but two other popes were still alive, whom Dante hated no less, perhaps even more, because they were his political enemies, the opponents or impediments of his political ideal, — Boniface VIII. and Clement V. By means of one of those astounding inventions, so many of which sprang from his fertile mind, he intertwined with this satire against Nicholas a satire against the other two. The simoniacal popes will all come into the same pit, and, coming one after the other, will force each other lower down. In this

way it happens that Nicholas is expecting the one and
prophesies the other's coming, whereby Dante again
has the advantage of placing his sarcasms in another's
mouth, thus adding to their power and effect. It is
a worthy predecessor of theirs that speaks and fore-
tells their shame. Pope Nicholas hears voices at the
edge of the pit, and he immediately thinks that it
must be Boniface coming to take his place and to
push him down. This eager expectation of the other
converts the prophecy into reality, and we already see
Pope Boniface VIII., too, head foremost in the pit,
moving his flaming soles about in the air. In this
way Dante knew how to avenge himself and to deal
out punishment, when he considered it just. But
after the mockery he rises to a feeling of moral ear-
nestness. It is no longer irony, but genuine pain
that rings from his words: " Ah, Constantine ! of
how much ill was mother . . . ," and this holy wrath
pleases his good guide, Virgil, who listens with ap-
proval to his disciple's words, and then takes him into
his arms, raises him to his breast, and carries him to
the top of the next bridge. That is just the reason
why Dante's satire is so magnificent, because of the
earnestness on which it is based. He is so bold, be-
cause he feels himself strong in faith. He does not
attack religion and ecclesiastical institutions ; on the
contrary, he defends the Church against its false shep-
herds. He reproves the bad popes, but bows rever-
ently before the Papacy, and deeply feels the shame
brought on it by Philip the Fair, although the direct
sufferer was one whom he placed in Hell.

From satire there naturally develops a comic ele-
ment, which had its place in the old legends and in

the French mysteries, where, after the gradual elimination of the moral intention, it gave birth to farce. With Dante laughter is still essentially an agent for punishment and correction, as in the former visions of Hell. The place for this comic element is the fifth *bolgia*, where the peculators are immersed in a sea of pitch. Here we have the scenes of the shade of the man of Lucca, which the devils are dragging along and throwing into the lake, and of Giampolo of Navarra, who deceives the devils themselves, whereupon they become entangled in a curious brawl and fall into the pitch (Inf. xxi., xxii.). These are humorous descriptions, such as we might expect at that time, rough and primitive in the expressions and images, now and again recalling the infernal kitchen of Fra Giacomino; but they are of a kind to become popular, and, in point of fact, the grotesque figures of the devils, especially, did become popular, — their names, Barbariccia, Libicocco, etc., occurring frequently in later Italian literature.

In the seventh *bolgia* (c. xxv.) occurs the description of the transformation of men into serpents, and serpents into men, which has always been admired as an extraordinary feat of the imagination. And such, indeed, it is. At the same time it appears to me that the effect does not correspond entirely to the means employed. This description is too minute to be fantastic, and the imagination demands greater freedom of treatment in the case of matters that entirely transcend the limits of the natural; being shackled by so many details, it remains inactive and does not really represent the marvel to itself, with the result that the effect produced is grotesque rather than fantastic, as is the case here. I do not mean that even such an effect is wasted; on the contrary, it is well adapted to regions of the comic and grotesque, like the *Malebolge*. All I maintain is that this transformation should not be given out as one of Dante's greatest creations. Farinata on his bed of fire, the celestial messenger traversing the Stygian marsh dry-shod, Pope Nicholas in the infernal *borsa* are splendid creations of Dante's imagination. The eighth *bolgia* (c. xxvi.), again, supplies us with a picture loftier in character, — Ulysses, the immortal type of man's thirst for knowledge, in whose bold voyage of discovery Dante has managed to express all the strange poetry of the sea.

The deeper we descend, the more crude and realistic does the style become: Dante does not hesitate to present to us objects that are ugly, and to call them by their proper name. The sojourn of the forgers in the tenth *bolgia* (c. xxix. *seq.*) is the place of the most loathsome things, of diseases, wounds, and stench, and the poet does not spare his colors; on the contrary, he paints for us, intentionally and with various images, the most disgusting objects. He also describes to us the quarrel between Master Adam of Brescia and the Greek Sinon. They come to blows and hurl vulgar imprecations at each other, so that Virgil is almost angry with the poet for listening: —

For a base wish it is to wish to hear it.

Further on even this ceases; every kind of movement ceases. In the ninth and last circle the very nature of Hell has become ice, and the sinners are frozen in ice. Here treachery is punished, the deepest corruption of the human mind. Against this black-

est of sins the heart is closed, for these condemned
souls there is naught but cruel hatred. Dante ill-
treats them, and ruthlessly treads on them with his
feet. Higher up he gave the souls promises of fame,
in order to make them speak. But these down here
do not wish people in the world to speak of them:
they cannot expect glory, but only infamy. Accord-
ingly, they do not wish to speak, and to say who they
are; but Dante endeavors to make them do it by force,
nay, even by deception. He finds in the ice Bocca
degli Abati, who betrayed the Guelfs in the battle
of Monteaperti. When he gives no reply to the ques-
tion as to who he is, the poet's wrath is kindled: he
seizes him by the hair, and begins shaking him so
that he howls, with his eyes turned down (xxxii. 97).
In this trait of savage cruelty towards the sinner,
towards the soul abandoned by Divine grace, there is
something magnificent in the very barbarism, that
shows us Dante as the man of his age, with his piti-
less conception of justice. But, none the less, even
in the midst of this icy desert, here at the very end of
Hell, where every feeling would seem to be dead, ap-
pear once again all the poetic elements that we found
in such numbers in the upper circles. In the scene of
Ugolino the entire poetic character of Dante's Hell is
revealed again; it forms, as it were, a final synthesis
of this Hell, with all its horrors and emotions. Never
was a more terrible spectacle invented by a poet. Here
Divine justice has made the injured one himself the
instrument for punishing the criminal, and handed the
sinner over to the man he has sacrificed, so that the
latter may avenge himself; and Ugolino satisfies his
boundless wrath by gnawing away the skull of his

enemy, the Archbishop Ruggieri. But, on being questioned by Dante, this shade opens its mouth to speak, and tells us its story, — this, too, from motives of revenge; however, it is a story of tender feelings, which, being wounded in bestial fashion, have become the cause of this bestial revenge.